GREETINGS
TOP OF THE POPS
VIEWERS!!

Welcome to this, your very own Top Of The Pops Annual 1992 – an indispensable volume packed with gasp-worthy pop features on all your favourite pop stars. Sigh! at the shimmering pop posters to adorn your wall. Wonder! at the incredible wisdom of the stars' 'revelations'. Ponder! at the Radio 1 DJs' lifestyles. Chortle! at the many jolly jokes within... and much more.

● This is your very own annual so we don't want it to be stolen by some envious pal at the bus stop – so fill in your details to flummox them. Haw!

NAME:..

AGE:...

ADDRESS:..

....

....

TOP OF THE POPS IS GREAT BECAUSE

....

....

MY FAVOURITE POP STAR IS:...............................

AND MY POEM ABOUT THEM GOES LIKE THIS

....

....

....

....

cont

ents...

"My nickname
in my family
was The Mouth."

"If I had nothing to do I would stay in the gym forever."

MADONNA

"If I have a 7.00am call for a movie, I'll get up at 4.30 to exercise. If I don't, I'll never forgive myself."

▲ Madonna and Warren Beatty go to the opening of their movie *Dick Tracy*.

"There are still those people, who no matter what I do will always think of me as a little disco tart."

★

"I have to schedule everything and that drives everyone I'm with insane. *Everyone*. They go, 'Can't you just wake up in the morning and not plan your day? Can't you just be spontaneous?' And I just can't."

★

"My first boyfriend was when I was 14 or 15. He was the only boy who would dance with me in school because I was really wild at the high school dances and I danced completely insanely. So he won my heart because he wasn't afraid of me."

"When I was growing up I was religious in a passionate adolescent way. Jesus Christ was like a movie star, my favourite idol of all."

"I sometimes think I was born to live up to my name. How could I be anything else but what I am having been named Madonna? I would have either ended up a nun or this."

★

"My whole life is in a constant state of disarray, and the one thing that doesn't change is the work-out. If I had nothing to do I would stay in the gym forever. If you've failed in every way in your day, you've accomplished one thing — you've gotten through your work-out!"

● "I do what I want. I'm the boss."

▲ Madonna with very famous clothes designer Jean-Paul Gaultier. He designed the costumes for Madonna's BLOND AMBITION tour.

"I have an iron will. And all of my will has always been to conquer some horrible feeling of inadequacy. I've always struggled with that fear. Because even though I've become Somebody, I still have to prove that I'm *Somebody*. My struggle has never ended and it probably never will."

▲ Madonna in her video *Vogue*.

"It's a really hard thing to accept that no matter what you do you can't change a person. You want to think that if this person is in love with you, you have control over them. But you don't. And to accept that in life is next to impossible."

MADONNA

"I always knew I was going to have a special life."

▲ Madonna in the video for *Like A Prayer*.

"You could watch this documentary and say 'I still don't know the real Madonna' and good. Because you will never know the real me. Ever."

★

"I never take any time off if I can help it. I've taken three week-long vacations in the last ten years."

"I believe in God, I believe that everything you do comes back to you. I believe in the innate goodness of people and the importance of that."

"I look around and go 'God, it's great. I have fame and fortune'. But then I see Mia Farrow on the set with her baby, and I think she seems absolutely content. She has a huge family, and that just seems like the most important thing. And, you know, love and everything. I don't really have that, but time hasn't run out for me yet."

▲ Madonna and her ex-husband, movie star Sean Penn.

"If I do something and there's 100 people in the room and 99 people say they liked it, I only remember the person who didn't like it."

★

"People have this idea that if you're sexual and beautiful and provocative then there's nothing else you could possibly offer. People have *always* had that image of women."

★

"I wonder if I could ever find a man like me. . . If I did I'd probably kill him."

8

▲ Madonna and her pal Michael Jackson at the *Oscars*.

"I'll never learn patience."

MICHAEL JACKSON'S ZOO!!

How would you like to share your house with a llama called Louie? Would you be pleased to find a python wound round the taps at bath-time? Well, if you would, your name is probably Michael Jackson and you're the sort of chap who likes animals so much that you have a complete menagerie in your back garden!

① BUBBLES THE CHIMP

Latin name: Pan Satyrus
Comes from near the Niger and Congo rivers in Central Africa. The male is about five feet high and weighs 110 pounds. Likes to mimic people and ride bikes and drink tea (good lad) and is highly smart all round, even though its brain is only a third the size of a human's. Its arms reach right down to its knees. Usually only has one baby, though can have twins, and lives 'til it's about forty years old.

② A MACAW

Latin name: Ara
A sort of very big, long-tailed parrot found in areas from Mexico and the West Indies down to Paraguay. The best ones to keep are the blue and yellow ones (*ara macao*) or the red and blue ones (*ara araruna*), but none of them talk, they just make a horrid screeching sound.

③ MUSCLES, THE EIGHT FOOT PYTHON

Latin name: Pythoninae
Also known as boa constrictor (*Lat: constrictor constrictor*), kills prey by wrapping round them and squashing them to death (ugh). Can kill animals as big as leopards and wild boar. Indian python can grow up to 15 feet long, African up to 25. Lays between 50 and 100 eggs at a time and then coils around them till they hatch, so they can't be all that "BAD" (geddit haw haw *haw* – sorry).

④ SEVERAL FAWNS

Latin name: Dama Dama
They look like Bambi and are really little fallow deer, reddish brown on top with white spots. They're 35 inches tall at the shoulder when they're fully grown i.e. they're quite weedy really.

⑤ SOME DEER

Latin name: Cervidae
Biggest is the elk or moose, whose antlers can be 11 feet in span and which stand six feet high at shoulder. Some little deer, like the springbok from South Africa, protect themselves by boinging high in the air when they're threatened.

10

A GIRAFFE

Latin name: Giraffa
Grow to 19 feet tall. Skin on hindquarters is thicker than rhino hide! Are generally silent, shy and inoffensive, though can kick in all directions when threatened. Can use tongue almost like a hand in pulling off leaves to eat.

LOUIE THE LLAMA

Latin name: Lama Glama
Is really just a camel without a hump from South America. Lives in herds. Very shy animal, but if you annoy it, it'll spit at you (ho). Wild ones are brown on top and whitish below and domestic ones, particularly alpacas, are bred for their wool.

BEN THE RAT

Latin name: Rattus
Brown (*rattus norvegicus*) are the most common, although black ones (*rattus rattus*) are also found. Can chew through lead piping and concrete in a few hours. Normally live in groups and can have up to six litters of six babies *every year*. Live for about five years.

RICKY THE PARROT

Latin name: Psittaciformes
The best talker is the Scarlet-tailed African grey parrot (*psitacus erithacus*) which is intelligent and can live up to 50 years. The next best is the Blue-fronted Amazon parrot (*amazona aestiva*) from South America.

DJ

NICKY CAMPBELL

"I have too many favourite pop stars to write a poem about one."

Full name: Nicky Campbell
Date of birth: 1.4.61
Starsign: Aries
Birthplace: Edinburgh
Height: 6'0"
Weight: 11 stone, 8 pounds
Colour of eyes: Blue
Do you have any pets: No, but I love dogs.
What qualifications do you have: An Honours Degree in History.
Describe your house: "Home".
What are your parents' jobs: Both retired – my father was a publisher.
Do you have any brothers and sisters and what are they like: I've one sister, five years older than me – she's nothing like me, very pleasant!
Where's your favourite holiday place: The Scottish Highlands and Italy.
If you weren't a super DJ, what would you be: Er... I suppose I'd be a bad one, wouldn't I?
When was the last time you cried: When I went to see the film *Dead Poets Society* – I had to pay four people in.
Most embarrassing moment on Top Of The Pops: My very first appearance was embarrassing, terrifying, nerve-racking and great fun.
Tell us a joke: The English Cricket Team.
What's in your pockets right now: House keys, car keys, crumpled 5 pound note, half a packet of wine gums.
Write a poem about your favourite pop star: I have too many favourite pop stars to write a poem about one – it would end up as a volume of poetry!
Do you like yourself: I've got to, haven't I? I'm the best I've got!
Do you have a message for the readers: Keep watching Top Of The Pops – the best music programme on British TV, of course!

12

★ **KIM** APPLEBY

"We're more a family than a business."

★

NEW KIDS ON THE BLOCK

Joe: "The only real friends I have are my crazy low-life friends back in Boston."

Donnie: "That image stuff sucks. Why can't people just be people?"

YO !

Jordan (on the 'official' New Kids cartoon): "My cartoon has an upper lip. No one has an upper lip in the cartoon except me 'cos I asked for an upper lip – which makes me look like I've got really big lips!"

★

Donnie: "When I'm not on tour I don't feel like I'm doin' nothin'. I feel like I'm letting my career just slip away from me. I never rest on my laurels."

Jordan (on their immense fame): "I expected exactly what came. Even when the first album died I went round and told people, 'Yeah, man, we're gonna be famous. I probably won't be in school next year. I'll probably have a tutor.'"

 Jon: "There's lots of nice smells. Pine trees. Our bodyguard's cologne. He always smells nice. He won't be hummin'."

Jon: "The secret of the universe is that we're all going to die one day because there's too much pollution."

⭐ Jon: "I almost never sing lead vocals, and it doesn't bother me. With us knowing each other so long, we're more a family than a business."

⭐ Jordan: "I feel really lucky that there are five of us. If one of us was solo and it got this big it would be very, very hard to handle."

Danny: "I met this older lady in L.A. She was 30. She was from the Philippines and didn't know who I was or nothing. We talked and I invited her to eat with us. She was sitting in the car and I said 'You're very pretty, you know that?' And she said 'You're very handsome,' and I'm gonna be honest, no one's ever called me handsome, and that was the most flattering thing anyone's ever said to me."

Donnie: "I can't understand why people make so much fuss over being a pop star. They weren't born special. They weren't born famous. They're just ordinary dudes. That's what I am. I can never forget that I came from nowhere with nuthin' in my pockets."

Danny: "Our voices are our instruments."

Jordan: "Fans shouldn't say we can't date. That's taking away our human rights."

NEW KIDS ON THE BLOCK

Jon: "I've never lived with a girl. I'm not at an age where I want to have a real girlfriend. One person for the rest of my life? That's ridiculous. If I was to date someone, she'd have to be a lot older, like 19 or 20."

Donnie: "We're getting lynched, man. Why is it such a crime that we're 'only singers'? Did Frank Sinatra write his own songs or play any instruments?"

Jon: "We never have roadies pick out girls for us. How'd the other girls feel?"

Danny: "I just hang and sometimes I just goof and sometimes I'm just not with it, y'know?"

Jon: "You guys should get down with the ice in that country (i.e. Britain). None of your drinks are cold!"

DONNIE

Donnie: "Oh, man, I got more girls liking me than I ever had in my life. When you have a few million girls who really like you, you don't want to disappoint them. But if I see a girl, and I wanna meet her, I'm gonna meet her."

Jordan: "At home I cannot walk down my own little street. On the road, I can't even go out in the hallway of a hotel. Some days it gets to me pretty bad. If I want to go out at night, I go to a punk club where they don't care who I am."

JON

Danny: "I'm looking for girls! I just want girls I can hang out with, I've tried commitment on the road and it didn't work out, so if you want commitment don't come looking at me."

Jon: "When all else fails, we can always play Vegas."

N K
O
T B

Jordan: "People get us wrong. They think we're white kids from white neighbourhoods who liked rock and roll and then here comes some black guy from the ghetto and we're like, 'Gee, how do you sing like Luther Vandross? Teach me how to dance like you black guys'. It wasn't like that. We're city kids. I've been breakdancing and listening to rap music since I was a little kid."

Danny: "I'm on a diet. I have a trainer and a nutritionist. And I'm coming out with a body building and nutrition book next year."

DJ

GARY DAVIES

"Roses are red
Violets are blue
There's no better
band than
U2."

Full name: Gary Davies
Date of birth: 13.12.57
Starsign: Sagittarius
Place of birth: Manchester
Height: 5′ 10″
Weight: 11 stone, 7 pounds
Colour of eyes: Hazel
Do you have any pets: A brother called Mark!
What qualifications do you have: 3 O Levels and a gold swimming medal.
Describe your house: Four walls, three bedrooms and a kitchen (rarely used).
What are your parents' jobs: I'm not telling you!
Do you have any brothers and sisters and what are they like: I've got one brother and two sisters and they're all much better looking than me.
Where's your favourite holiday spot: My Radio 1 studio.
If you weren't a super DJ, what would you be: Unhappy.
When was the last time you cried and why: When Manchester United got knocked out of the F.A. Cup.
What was your most embarrassing moment on Top Of The Pops: My very first appearance on Top Of The Pops, when I had to wear a Radio 1 jacket which was three sizes too small for me.
Tell us a joke: What's the last thing that goes through a bee's mind when it hits a car windscreen? Its bum!!
What's in your pockets right now: £3.45, a pair of glasses, four CDs, two 12″ records, a record player, a pair of headphones and an old ski pass.
Write a poem about your favourite pop star:
Roses are red
Violets are blue
There's no better band than U2.
Do you like yourself: Only when I'm asleep.
Do you have a message for the readers: If you believe all this you've got problems!! P.S. Thanks for watching Top Of The Pops!

★ **JANET** JACKSON

"This front bit of my hair is my beak. Without my beak I wouldn't be Vanilla Ice."

"I love my mother but I'm not close to her and I hardly ever see her or talk to her no more. I talked to her once last month. I don't have time. I don't see any friends. Nobody but my crew and reporters."

"There are just too many girls. . ."

VANILLA ICE

"When I was at high school we used to have battles on street corners and breakdancing was part of that scene. In the beginning I copied the black kids but most of what I picked up from them was attitude; the way they moved and acted. I soon realised that to stand out I had to be original. I became a trendsetter and was soon burnin' up the streets with my dancin'."

⭐

"It's incredibly easy getting girls. There are just too many girls to choose from."

⭐

"Nothing like me has ever happened in the rap world *ever*. There's a lot of reasons why I'm better than the other rappers. It's the rappin', I'm something that you don't see every day."

⭐ ⭐ ⭐

"The girls manhandle me badly, man. In Miami 5,000 kids skipped school so they could come and see me and they all attacked me. They ripped all of my clothes completely off! Well. . . they didn't, not everything. They couldn't rip my shorts off 'cos they were made of nylon. Actually it was lucky I had a pair of shorts on because usually I don't wear anything underneath."

"I don't think I'm God or anything like that."

"Yeah, I was stabbed. I woke up in hospital almost dead. But I didn't die and I believe God gave me a second chance. That's when I said 'Yo Ice, you're doin' wrong. The streets ain't cool, gangs ain't cool, drugs ain't cool, and you can't speak knowledge.' So I tell everyone to stay in school 'cos that's cool."

⭐

"My bedroom on my bus has got mirrors all around it, it's got blue neon lights, a compact disc player right there next to my bed and what else? Got a little chandelier at the top of it and it's got a biiiig roooound beeed. Nope, I'm not joking."

"My favourite phrases are 'Chillin' like Bob Dylan' and 'Maxin' like Michael Jackson' and 'Livin' like Thanks Givin'."

"As far as seeing colours in terms of my soul and people, I'm colour blind. I'm not a white guy having to be black in other words. If the world was colour blind there'd be no racism."

⭐

"Oh, I used to be the serious Mr Dare! I'd do whatever people dared me to do. I was nuts. I was tough, crazy and dumb. But that's what got me into this business. My friend went and entered me for this rap competition in Dallas and I said, 'No, man. I'm the only white guy here. These people don't want me in here.' So he goes, 'I dare you'. I thought, 'Oh, man, a dare. I can't resist!' So I got up and here I am. So thanks friend!"

AMAZING FACTS ABO

● The very first edition of Top Of The Pops was broadcast live (in black and white!) on New Year's Day 1964 at 6.36pm.

● It was recorded in a converted church in Manchester and Jimmy "Now then now then uheuheuheuh etc" Savile was the presenter.

● The original producer of TOTP was called Johnnie Stewart and he devised certain basic rules which the show has followed ever since. For example, he was the one who first decided that the No. 1 record must always appear at the end of the show.

● Here are the other rules: a) The highest new entry and the highest climbing record should be played whenever possible.
b) Never play the same disc on consecutive weeks, unless it's the No. 1 or it was one of last week's "Breakers".
c) Never play a disc which is going down the charts, unless. . .
d) . . . it "bounces back" i.e. it climbs higher than its original position.
e) Non-movers are counted as having dropped, unless they stay at the same place for four weeks – then it's up to the Producer to decide whether or not to have them on again.

● In 1967, Top Of The Pops moved to the Lime Grove studios in London.

● Also in '67, the Top Of The Pops Orchestra (!) made its first appearance. It provided the backing-track for the singers to mime to during transmission.

● Because some bands couldn't appear on TOTP and didn't have a video to show, in 1964 a dance group (hurrah!) was introduced to throw a few interesting shapes to a record being played without a group.

● *Jo Cook's Go-Jo's* were the first of these ace dance groups and regularly grooved along with gay abandon until they were replaced by first, *Pan's People*, *Ruby Flipper*, then *Legs & Co* and finally *Zoo*.

● They're not on anymore (boooo) because their costumes and set cost too much. And also because sometimes they'd prepare a dance to a song and it would then plummet down the charts, leaving them with only a very short time to devise a new routine before the show!

UT TOP OF THE POPS

● There have been four – four! – different theme tunes to Top Of The Pops.

● They are: a) a percussion piece by Johnnie Stewart and Harry Rabinowitz.
b) CCS's version of a song called *A Whole Lotta Love* by Led Zeppelin (squealy guitars, dramatic drums).
c) *Yellow Pearl* (another rock-out rouser) by Phil Lynott of Thin Lizzy.
d) *The Wizard* by Paul Hardcastle (the current theme).

● Despite the fact that Top Of The Pops is such a hugely popular show and involves so much work, there's only ever three people in the Top Of The Pops office – the Producer, the Production Assistant and the Assistant Floor Manager.

● The longest time a record has stayed at No. 1 in the official chart is 9 weeks.

● Three records have done this: *Bohemian Rhapsody* by Queen in 1975; *Mull Of Kintyre* by Wings in the winter of 1977 through to the New Year of 1978; and *You're The One That I Want* by John Travolta and Olivia Newton-John in 1978. So now you know.

● The show was only meant to run for six weeks but has lasted for so long now (twenty-seven years) that it is older than forty per cent of its viewers. Cor blimey!

● The first proper industry "chart" appeared on 12 February 1969.

● Before that, folk from the *NME*, *Melody Maker*, *Record Mirror* and *Disc* made unofficial charts by phoning up a few record stores to find out which records were selling the best. Hardly very accurate, so the system was changed – shops had to keep diaries of exactly which discs they had sold every week.

● On 4 January 1983, the all-new Gallup chart was introduced. Computerized and with a digital time system so you could check that the records were actually being sold, the store owners phoned in their results (called "returns") which were checked against the computer count and processed at a much faster rate. The same system is used today.

● Top Of The Pops is completely ace. And brill.

FACTFILE

ANTHEA TURNER

"'Poets (and John Lennon) are the unacknowledged legislators of the world' – by Anthea "Shelley" Turner."

Full name: Anthea Turner
Date of birth: 25.5.61
Starsign: Gemini
Place of birth: Stoke-on-Trent
Height: 5'6"
Weight: 8½ stone
Colour of eyes: Green
Do you have any pets: A dog called Tom and a pony called Caramac.
What qualifications do you have: 7 'O' Levels, 2 'A' Levels.
Describe your house: Uncomplicated and peaceful.
What are your parents' jobs: My Dad's a company director and Mum's a teacher.
Do you have any brothers and sisters and what are they like: I've got one sister called Wendy who's a TV & radio scriptwriter.
Where's your favourite holiday spot: Grenada.
If you weren't a super presenter, what would you be: A magazine editor.
When was the last time you cried and why: When I ran a door over my bare toes – the pain brought tears to my eyes.
What was your most embarrassing moment on Top Of The Pops: Calling The KLF The KLM. . . KLM is a Dutch airline.
Tell us a joke: What's green, has eight legs and if it fell from a tree it would kill you? A snooker table.
What's in your pockets right now: Car keys, a ten pound note, *Barclay* card, 5p (which has been in forever), *W.H. Smith* receipt.
Write a poem about your favourite pop star: Poets (and John Lennon) are the unacknowledged legislators of the world – by Anthea "Shelley" Turner.
Do you like yourself: Yes I do actually.
Do you have a message for the readers: Hold on to this book forever. It reflects an era in your life that one day you'll crack up over.

★ **CHESNEY** HAWKES

TOP OF THE POPS

★ fashion fuddler

Pop stars eh? They're some dressers, aren't they? The following clues describe the chosen style signatures of seven pop people. Fill them in and you'll reveal a mean 'n' hairy rock combo from the US. Cor!

1. "Unusual" hair that extends upwards into a crown above his head and seems like it's part of his googly-eyed face plus short trousers, a catapult and a T-shirt that reads "Underachiever".
2. *Timberland* boots, denim shirts and trousers, usually carries a guitar.
3. Personalized "beak" hairdo, strangely shaved eyebrows, wobble-free jawline and "trademark" spooky hand shape.
4. Long straight blonde hair, leather trousers and plenty of "attitude".
5. All of this Manchester band sport baggy trousers, dodgy haircuts and "oh dear I'm about to fall over" expressions. (Especially Bez.)
6. Smart suits, jet black hair and gangly limbs add up to Britain's "Top Light Entertainer" who "wouldn't let it lie".
7. Interesting wigs, 70s "gear". . . bit of a change from the curly-topped *Neighbour* of yore.

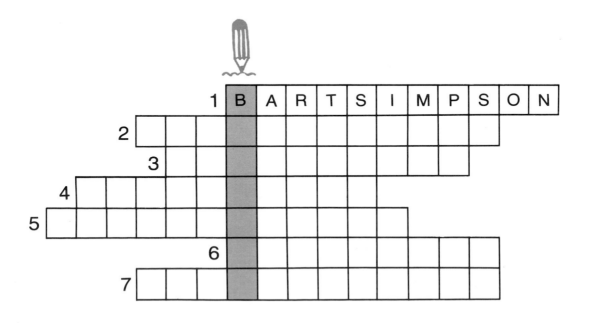

1 | B | A | R | T | S | I | M | P | S | O | N

● **The hidden rawk and roll curly locked "muthas" are · · · / · · · ·**

difficult height teaser ★

Pop stars come in all shapes and sizes, don't they? Tall and gangly of limb, short and stocky, round of face and body. . . there's so many types. Here are the heights of nine of them. See if you can work out which pop star is which height by using the four clues below. Write their name in the box next to the appropriate measurement. It's a toughie!

1. Although Gloria is quite small, she's still taller than Janet Jackson. She's smaller than Wendy James though, and Shaun Ryder's taller than the lot of them.
2. If Donnie was 2″ taller, he'd be as tall as Craig.
3. Matt may be taller than Craig but he's still 1″ smaller than Mike from Jesus Jones.
4. If Danny was 1″ taller he'd be Shaun Ryder's height and if Shaun was 2″ taller he'd be as tall as Donnie.

JANET JACKSON	5′1″
	5′2″
	5′5″
	5′7″
	5′8″
	5′10
	6′
	6′1″
	6′2″

Mike from Jesus Jones

Donnie Wahlberg

Craig McLachlan

Janet Jackson

Gloria Estefan

Matt Goss

Shaun Ryder

Danny Wood

Wendy James

Picture Puzzler ★

These jolly drawings are more than they seem. . . for they are in fact clues to some of the nation's top pop types! Can you guess them?

● **Turn To Page 61 For The Answers**

"I guess I'm known for my baggy pants."

MC HAMMER

"When I was young I was very, very, very small. Up until the senior year in high school I didn't even cross the five foot mark. Then in one year I shot up a foot. But I had a big wad of a head. A big jug head; a little skinny body and a big old man's head."

"I played baseball in college. I've had a couple of pro try-outs but I'm not disappointed that I didn't carry on because I make more money and get more visibility doing this."

"I used to go to church six days a week. Unfortunately I don't always have the time any more."

"God blessed me with persistence, caring and confidence. It's not really me that makes it happen. All my characteristics have been given to me by God."

!

"I've got over 1,000 outfits."

"Do I get a lot of love offers? Well yeah, sure. And what's my answer? Oh come on, I'm too busy."

★

"My records do change people's lives. They continually come up and tell me so."

★

"I think with the grace of God I will be here for a long time."

"I don't want to be number two. I worked hard to be number one and that's where I want to stay."

★

"I couldn't care what the next rap artist thinks of me. . . I stand alone. Everything about me is untypical. I don't require the approval of other rappers. They bore me."

★

"I guess I am known for my baggy pants."

★

"I have 65 employees depending on me to do my thing so that we can all keep going. We all stick together and make sure things go smoothly. Things can get really tough, but we all pace ourselves and make sure we eat properly, rest and keep fit."

"Before I did a video I tried to think of all my moves and I came up with 80 different dances."

DJ

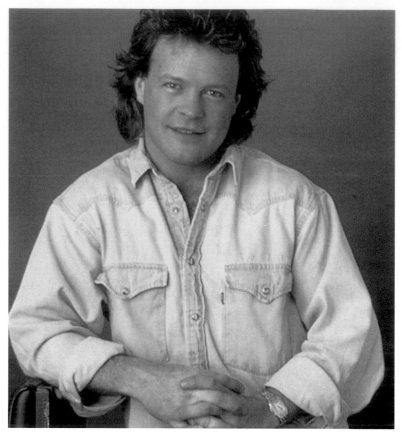

BRUNO BROOKES

"Oh Kylie, Oh Kylie,
Oh Kyle
You've been making
hits for a while
I should be so lucky
'Cos you are the best
If you would come
be my neighbour
And wash my vest."

Full name: Bruno Brookes (real name Trevor)
Date of birth: 24.4.59
Starsign: Taurus
Place of birth: Stoke-On-Trent
Height: 5′ 6″ and a half
Weight: 10 stone
Colour of eyes: Blue
Do you have any pets: 1 cat called Harry, 1 dog called Jesse and some marine fish.
What qualifications do you have: Common sense.
Describe your house: Homely and unfurnished.
What are your parents' jobs: Mum's an MD (i.e. Managing Director) and Dad's a headmaster.
Do you have any brothers and sisters and what are they like: Three brothers called Lloyd, Zac and Lindon – they're all great.
What's your favourite holiday spot: Ireland and Rome.
If you weren't a super DJ, what would you be: A rubbish DJ! Actually, I'd probably be an architect or some kind of designer.
When was the last time you cried and why: Two weeks ago – I was cutting an onion.
What was your most embarrassing moment on Top Of The Pops: Doing the whole show with a black mark on my nose and nobody told me about it.
Tell us a joke: How many DJs does it take to change a lightbulb? 1.21112212.
What's in your pockets right now: A credit card and some fluff.
Write a poem about your favourite pop star:
Oh Kylie, Oh Kylie, Oh Kyle
You've been making hits for a while
I should be so lucky
'Cos you are the best
If you would come
be my neighbour
And wash my vest.
Do you like yourself: Er. . . sometimes!
Do you have a message for the readers: No music show beats Top Of The Pops.

★ **DANNII** MINOGUE

MATT + LUKE

Bros. They came, they conquered the pop universe for two big years and then they got completely ripped off, ended up with hardly any money, and the press said they were down and outs. Now they're back! Hoorah!! with nice new haircuts and a "philosophical" outlook and Matt's finally got himself a proper girlfriend and everything's thoroughly "wicked". And this is how they did it. . .

MATT

● **He was really quite skint for a while. . .**
"Well, let's face it, a lot of money went on what you call service things, like lawyers and accountants, and all the people you need to take care of business and about a hundred thousand went on touring, which is what any band pays. But more than anything we were ripped off by a whole load of people who made a pile of money out of us and then turned their backs on us. We were just really naive – even though we genuinely believed we weren't – but we weren't quite as penniless as the press made out – we never starved, put it that way."

● **He is still in the same house and there's still Brosettes mobbing the front door. . .**
"I nearly was evicted, yeah! But I hung on and it's alright now. There still are Brosettes but they don't hang around and stuff anymore, they're like friends now, wondering what's happening, when the new records are coming out. But they've grown up a lot, too, of course, they've got boyfriends and jobs and all that. Mind you, there were 600 of them outside my house on my birthday – so they still bother enough for things like that!"

● **They think they're more exciting than the pop stars of today. . .**
"There aren't real pop stars anymore. Vanilla Ice. . .weeeell, naah. EMF I like, they're quite exciting, but so many of the rest of them are like 'ooo we're not pop stars, oh no, we're just doing a job or we're just normal' and all this and you think 'well, I'm a pop star and I'm proud of it!' It's been a dream for people since time began to be a pop star, y'know live out some kind of a fantasy life and I think 'yeah! I'm well lucky! If I'm going to be a pop star I'm going to be an exciting one and be proud of it!'

"If I'm going to be a pop star, I'm going to be an exciting one, and be proud of it. . ."

● **He's still wearing dandy threads of the snoot variety. . .**

"Snoot clothes? Heh heh, yeah, well that's just what we've always liked, we couldn't exactly come back with loads of Soul II Soul beats on the album and hip clothes, could we? We're not hip people, we're not a hip band, we're not EMF and we're not De La Soul. We're just us."

● **He's got a new haircut. . .**

"No I haven't!"

Yes you have, it's all sweepy.

"Naaah, just combed it over a bit that's all!"

● **He's finally got himself a proper girlfriend. . .**

"Yeah! Yeah. . .heh heh. 'Course I'm not tellin' you her name. She's my girlfriend that's all I'm sayin'. Been going out for a year now. . . 'Course I love her, yeah. And I'm sure *The Sun* will have some revelations about it all."

● **They're going on tour again. . .**

"We'll definitely be touring in 1992, we're hoping to be touring by Christmas actually. According to our management and that we can still play the Arena an' stuff, y'know, the big venues, so that'll be brilliant. We can't wait!"

● **He's been buying spook-presents for his mum. . .**

"I bought my mum a crystal ball last Christmas actually. Quite a big one with loads of sort of triangular bits inside. She does use it. She can read tarot cards and stuff, too. I think I'm quite psychic too, actually, I just get strange feelings about things happening. My grandfather was a mystic and a faith healer, don't forget!"

LUKE

And here's Luke, he's on the car phone as usual, and he's got a new dog and a helicopter on his front lawn — good heavens. . .

● **He's got a boffin's car (and a boundy dog). . .**

"I'm in a Jag SS7 these days, it's a bit boffiny for me, bit square for me I think, but it's a nice car. I've got a dog now, y'see, so I have to have four doors in the car. Got a new dog, yeah! It's an Old English Sheepdog, a *Dulux* dog, yeah! Called Coco. . .yeah, she's well nice."

● **He's surrounded by "believers". . .**

"I think I have changed, not drastically, I'm probably a bit more serious than I was before — I've got cabin fever at the moment, just been in the studio! But we realized it was just us, y'know 'it's just me and you Matt', and the people that are around us now are believers, y'know, they're not just people who are around because it's exciting and a good living."

● **He thinks Seal's well "top". . .**

"I think Seal's brilliant, if you're gonna do dance stuff, do it like Seal does, make proper songs with great melodies and a great voice, of course, that's about all I've liked for ages to be honest. Some souly tracks, but that's about it."

● **He's still in lerve (gawd love 'im) and he's got a Gazza haircut (haw haw). . .**

"Still living in the same house with Shirl, she's great, sitting next to me at the moment, she says hello but she's half asleep heh heh. D'you like the haircut? Alright, innit? Took a lot of nerve to get it cut like that actually 'cos it's been the same for four years. I had it done months and months ago and then when we got our first new pictures done everyone thought I had a George Michael cut and I thought 'I had it done before him!' A Gazza cut? Aw, gimme a break! haven't got that line round the back heheh."

● **He's got a helicopter (and he knows how to use it — just). . .**

"Matty bought me that for Christmas, it's a remote control, about three and a half feet long, it's quite good, it's got a 12 horsepower engine, I can actually hover it now though it takes up to two years to learn to fly it. It depends on your co-ordination and I thought well, if I can't do this it'll be a total embarrassment 'cos as a drummer I'm supposed to have quite a bit of co-ordination heh heh — but I managed it! I've crashed it about fifteen times, though, it's such an expensive hobby, they cost about 800 pounds and every time it crashes the propellers get all messed up and that costs about 30 quid a time to fix — so if it hits the floor it just messes up completely. Little boy's toys — same as usual heheh."

● **He's as happy as a skylark on the wisp of a breeze (near enough). . .**

"If you'd asked me six months ago I'd have said I was about a million times unhappier than I thought I could ever have been, ridiculously unhappy, but now I'm just excited. I couldn't ask for more right now."

"I'm a cross between Barbarella, Princess Margaret and Barbie."

KYLIE

"I've got a really good short term memory and a terrible long term memory. When people ask what my earliest memory is I have to say it was when I was about 12."

"I'm probably the most easily bored person on earth — I have to change all the time."

SCHOOL:

"Throughout school I was pretty quiet and I was just going to settle to be a secretary."

"I believe that the crystals I wear, such as quartz and amethyst, have special powers. I don't know a lot about them, but I'm convinced they have a positive energy in them which can help you."

energy

E

"Michael (Hutchence, of INXS) has had a big influence on me in every way. I've become a better person with him I think. He's made me more outrageous. I know he didn't used to like the way I looked, which doesn't surprise me. . ."

"Oh, I was seeing Jason, we just denied it for a long time."

"I've been dubbed the 'bimbo blonde' but you can guarantee that I wouldn't still be here if I was a 'bimbo blonde'."

★

"Most of my friends are older than me and they still don't know where they're at. So why do people expect me to have the world worked out?"

★

"I don't mind talking to people or signing autographs when I'm out but please let me finish my meal first!"

★

"The more flying I do the more afraid I become of it. When I'm up in the air I'm always wondering how the plane manages to stay up there."

★

"I definitely want to have kids. . . I'd like two girls and a boy. I would never have just one kid because my dad was an only child and he hated it. I'd definitely put my kids before my career."

"I cringe when I watch myself on *Neighbours* because it's so old, but I also cringe when I watch really recent things of myself. I even hate to hear myself back on the radio."

"I believe that there are two of me. There's Kylie Minogue Ltd which is the all-singing, all-dancing person, and there's Kylie Minogue the quiet, shy person who likes to be at home."

"My biggest weakness is shoes. I've got about 100 pairs."

"I'm a cross between Barbarella, Princess Margaret and Barbie."

"It's hard to choose a guy who has every quality that I want in a man, but I consider Sean Connery, Lenny Kravitz and James from *Twin Peaks* to be sexy."

"Sometimes I can be dangerous to myself because I want to do everything, and I want to be responsible for everything which is not always a good idea."

"Smoking is gross! I don't like people who smoke cigarettes. I have to open the windows after Michael's been smoking in the house, but I don't send him out to the back garden – I'm not that extreme!"

"I just don't like my teeth and I'd like to swap them for better ones."

"I'm really interested in astronomy, organic food, homeopathy, aromatherapy, and a lot of the time I am a flower child."

"I'm proud that I'm a young woman. I'm proud of what I've done."

"On the surface it appears that there's a lot known about me but the beauty of it is that there's a lot that no one will ever know. I know that no matter what photos they take of me, paparazzi photos through the bathroom window, whatever it might be, they can't really get to you. They can't get to your soul."

"I was the girl next door, but she moved out and someone else moved in."

DJ

JAKKI BRAMBLES

"Frank, oh Frank
(Sinatra)
I'm glad you don't
work in a bank
Because I hear the
bells ring
When I hear you
sing
Songs for lovers
that swing."

Full name: Jakki Brambles
Date of birth: 1.3.67
Birthplace: Essex
Height: 5'4"
Weight: Not telling!
Colour of eyes: Greenish, greyish, blueish, they change all the time!
Do you have any pets: Only the two squirrels who live in my garden – they haven't got names yet I'm afraid.
What qualifications do you have: 8 'O' Grades, 3 Highers, 2 'A' Levels.
Describe your house: Spacious and sunny – it's out in the country which I love.
What are your parents' jobs: None of your business.
Do you have any brothers and sisters and what are they like: One big brother who's very big and very brotherly.
What's your favourite holiday place: California, Los Angeles.
If you weren't a super DJ, what would you be: A waster.
When was the last time you cried and why: That's none of your business, either!
Most embarrassing moment on Top Of The Pops: All of them – I'm a bit camera shy.
Tell us a joke: Me being called a super DJ!
What's in your pockets right now: Car keys and three pounds.
Write a poem about your favourite pop star:
Frank, oh Frank (Sinatra)
I'm glad you don't work in a bank
Because I hear the bells ring
When I hear you sing
Songs for lovers that swing
Do you like yourself: Occasionally.
Do you have a message for the readers: Go and buy a "Tree Shirt", *Oxfam* style, from *Dorothy Perkins* – and help plant a tree in Ethiopia.

40

★ **CLIFF** RICHARD

★ Pop stars and their pets

Many a pop starlet finds solace from the "trials" of fame in a cuddly companion (i.e. a pet). Do you know which pop star has which pet? Choose from a, b, or c.

BELINDA CARLISLE
a. Tree frog
b. Asian pot-bellied swayback pig
c. Long-haired white rabbit called Snookums

JANET JACKSON
a. Tarantula (particularly large, hairy and most unsavoury spider) called Dracula
b. Buffalo called Bertie
c. Anteater called Eugene

PAUL McCARTNEY
a. Hamster called Graham
b. Goat called Arlene
c. Lots of sheep

STEVIE V
a. Cat called Sherry
b. Antelope called Esmerelda
c. Fruit bat called Arthur

CRAIG McLACHLAN
a. Kangaroo called Cobblers
b. Dog called Bottom
c. Wild outback dingo called Wibbly

CHRIS LOWE (PET SHOP BOYS)
a. Yorkshire terrier called Boobles
b. Tortoise called Hubert
c. Badger called Gordon

CHESNEY HAWKES
a. Dog called Dizzy
b. Terrapin called Hawkeye
c. Gerbil called Daisy

JON KNIGHT (NEW KIDS)
a. Shar Pei dog called Nikko
b. Mongoose called Les
c. 3 ants called June, Wilbur and Zebulon

BETTY BOO
a. Boxer dog called Florence
b. Parrot called Monsieur Le Beak (because he's French)
c. 3 cats and a dog called Bobby

PAULA ABDUL
a. Cocker spaniel, a Pug and a Chihuahua called Rambo
b. Octopus called Donald
c. Stick insect called Ollie

★ pop geography

People come from everywhere all over the entire universe. Draw a line from the pop star's name to the place you think they come from (they're all jumbled up to confuse you completely haw haw. . .)

1. Seal
2. Rick Astley
3. Jordan Knight
4. Shaun Ryder (Happy Mondays)
5. Madonna
6. Betty Boo
7. Kylie Minogue
8. Paula Abdul
9. Derry (EMF)
10. Kim Appleby

a. Los Angeles, California
b. Hackney, East London
c. Warrington, Cheshire
d. Greater Manchester
e. Gloucester, West Country
f. Bay City, Detroit, U.S.A.
g. Melbourne, Australia
h. Paddington, London
i. Kensington, West London
j. Massachussetts, U.S.A.

tricky figure of 8

Write the answers to the questions below in the boxes provided and hey! you'll find that the shaded boxes provide the last letter of one answer and the first of the next! When everything's completed, unscramble the letters in the shaded boxes to reveal the name of an outrageous blonde pop star who's the lead singer of a "tuff" rock outfit. . .

1. -----/--- *You Baby?* wondered poor deserted Miss Boo.
2. Samba-ing sensation Gloria's last name.
3. Donnie, Danny, Joe and all the rest are, erm, *hangin' tough on the block* (poor lambs).
4. Irish singer with no hair and weepy eyes.
5. These Warriors gave us their definition of their boombastic jazz style.
6. The Queen Of Pop.
7. Lead singer of tougher than the rest Guns N' Roses.
8. This rabbit loved to *Swing The Mood* and begged us to *Come On Everybody*. Write his first name backwards for the answer.
9. This De Borg is the guitarist with Jesus Jones.
10. "------ is the colour of sunrays" remarked Soul II Soul in *Keep On Movin'* and they were not wrong. (NB It's also the colour of swoony Chesney's lovely locks.)

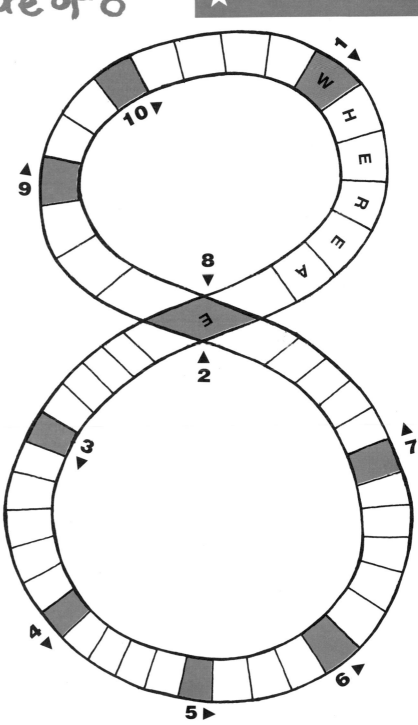

● **The unjumbled pop star is**

...../.....

● **Turn To Page 61 For The Answers**

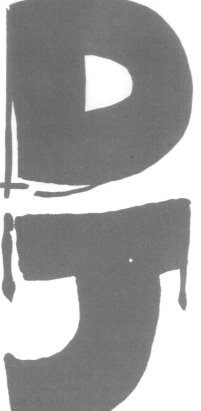

DJ

MARK GOODIER

"I'm hopeless at poems – sorry!"

Full name: Mark Goodier
Date of birth: 9.6.61
Starsign: Gemini
Place of birth: Salisbury, Rhodesia (now Zimbabwe)
Height: 5'11"
Weight: 12 stone
Colour of eyes: Blue
Do you have any pets: A golden Labrador called Faron.
What qualifications do you have: Very few, just many years of playing records.
Describe your house: A flat in North London with a small sunny garden and very bad decor – I've just moved in!
What are your parents' jobs: Mum's a conservationist and Dad's a teacher.
Do you have any brothers and sisters and what are they like: I've two really brainy brothers (both with degrees and nice haircuts).
Where's your favourite holiday spot: Skiing in Colorado – it's unbeatable.
If you weren't a super DJ what would you be: I'd still work in the music business, it's the only thing I know about.
When was the last time you cried and why: When I lost at *Nintendo*!
What was your most embarrassing moment on Top Of The Pops: When I realized my flies were undone — luckily nobody at home noticed!
Tell us a joke: Kid: Mummy, there's a man at the door with a bill. Mum: Don't be silly dear, it must be a duck with a hat on.
What's in your pockets right now: 46 pence, a huge bunch of keys and a half finished packet of *Polos*.
Write a poem about your favourite pop star: I'm hopeless at poems – sorry!
Do you like yourself: I'm not as fit as I used to be but generally I'm happy.
Do you have a message for the readers: Happy watching!

★ **PET** SHOP BOYS

WHAT DOES KYLIE'S

Or Madonna's big almond eyes? Or Chesney Hawkes' long chin? Or Donnie New Kid's blobby nose? According to a form of analysis (called Physiognomy) your personality is revealed in the shape of the things on your face. Let us peruse the evidence. . .

MADONNA

● Upwardly sloping eyebrows: This means that Madonna is a very smart person and is really good at "sussing out" what people are like. Eyebrows like this are often found on people who are original and creative in some way.

● Pouty lips. Full lips like this belong to people who are versatile, very passionate (especially in love) and thoroughly enjoy life. Her bottom lip is slightly thicker and this can indicate a love for "fun" foods.

● Almond-shaped eyes: Almond eyes are again a sign of wisdom and also that she enjoys being her own boss. They also show a hard-working person who thrives on discipline and a love for fitness and happiness through healthy living.

● Fleshy cheeks (with a hint of chiselled-ness): She has a mixture between a hard-working personality and someone who loves to go completely off her rocker now and again and have a good old knees-up and a hoot.

● Large nose: This is a leadership nose and one that says "live and let live!"

DONNIE WAHLBERG

● Blobby nose: This is a nose belonging to a sarcastic person who has a very dry wit. He's rebellious in an intelligent way and has very strong opinions indeed.

● Tiny 'n' smouldering eyes: These are very strong eyes, they indicate hidden manipulative tendencies (i.e. he's good at getting people to do things for him when they don't even realize!) and they also show he's quite romantic underneath his tough outward image.

● Eyebrows practically on top of his eyes: These eyebrows show intelligence and wisdom, but he can be quite neurotic sometimes.

● Square jaw: This indicates a desire for material things and he sees money as a form of power. He also has a higher than average awareness of his body when it comes to sensuality.

● "Stress" lines on the forehead: This shows a person who squeezes as much into life as he possibly can. He also feels naturally protective towards the weak. His whole face clearly spells "rebellion" with or without a cause, and he believes in communication.

EYEBROW REVEAL??

KYLIE MINOGUE

● Spooky right eyebrow: Kylie's right eyebrow arches up much higher than the left one which means the right side of her brain is more dominant than the left — and the right side is the one that makes you expressive and have lots of intuition.

● Rounded chin: This chin indicates a bright person who does things on impulse. A rounded chin can also mean someone who really likes practical jokes.

● Full lips: Kylie's got full lips which means she likes luxuries and is interested in spooky things like meditation, the spirit world and astrology. Her fuller bottom lip means she likes sweeties a lot.

● Big, slightly slanty eyes: Her eyes are quite almond-like and this shows she likes to be in control and be the boss.

● "Perfect" nose: This is a dreamer's nose — she followed the dreams and hopes she had when she was a child. You'll see her left eye is a slightly different size from the right one and this means she has two totally separate characters — one that's a young girl and the other an older woman. Oooer.

CHESNEY HAWKES

● Long chin (with a cleft in it): This is a chin that shows great tolerance and respect for other people and their opinions. He has patience, great wit and compassion and is prone to developing habits.

● Long nose: This shows he can be very thrifty with money, is quite a nosey person and likes to hide things in secret places.

● Almondish eyes (with a hint of beadiness): These eyes belong to someone who doesn't suffer fools gladly (i.e. if you're a buffoon he'll tell you), and is quick thinking. The beadiness aspect means he loves mischief and has a lot of ambition.

● Straight across eyebrows: These eyebrows mean Chesney likes to take life easy and likes his surroundings to be comfortable. He is also very perceptive and would know if you were telling a fib.

● Chiselled cheekbones: The classic chiselled cheekbones mean great pride and honesty. He has a very fresh face (as does Kylie) and this indicates a person who is very open, friendly and loves other people. Aw.

"People are scared of good looks."

EMF

Derry: (on the Forest): "People think we all live in trees or caves but it's really good here – lots of parties and everything."

★

Derry: "Our first gig was played in a pub — the sort of place where all the blokes are called things like One-Armed Les."

Ian: "We're into this as a lifestyle."

Ian: "We met as a drinking crew, all lads together. We'd all been in bands before so we could all play but what we wanted out of it was a laugh. Not everybody wants to wear a suit and worry about everything there is to worry about."

All: "People are scared of good looks."

Derry: "What would it take to get us to work with Pete Waterman? A pint of lager."

★

Derry: "We never argue anymore 'cos we've got other people to buy us drinks now. That's all we ever used to argue about, whose round it was. Now we don't have to worry about that."

Derry: "There was our legendary Afghan coat phase. . ."

Derry: "From our experience there's loads of 14-year-olds going to gigs now and all they want to do is go absolutely ape. They've had enough of Kylie and Jason."

★

Ian: "If I were a sound I'd be something really girly like the sound of raindrops. I'm a bit like that. I like pretty things."

★

Derry: "At the EMI conference we all got on the roof and stole the EMI flag and bent the flagpole. Didn't mean to, mind. . ."

Zac: ". . . Three o'clock in the morning and we're all diving in the swimming pool fully clothed, armed with fire extinguishers. Then the gold discs went missing of course. . ."

★

Derry: "It has been hard and it's understandable if people have a go. We've done so much press, every time someone opens a paper there's EMF. Because we appeal to a teeny-bop audience, mature artists assume we're just on a ride and that we won't be around next year. We'll definitely be around next year because we're a band and that's what people are overlooking."

Derry: "I'd sell my mum for a bunch of bananas."

the Betty Boo Story *

On 6 March 1970 a tiny wee girlie was born in West London to a Scottish office manager called Lisbeth and a train inspector fellow from Kuala Lumpur in Malaysia called John. They called her Alison Clarkson and were well chuffed with their lot. But not for long! For Alison, it seemed, was to be a trifle "troublesome". Alison's first memory is of her very first day at primary school. "I had a little kilt on, woolly tights, and a polo neck jumper," she recalls, "and I fell over and had a huge hole in my tights. I remember my leg being scabby for weeks." Oh dear. Alison was already a big pop music fan and grew up in a house full of all sorts of 60s and 70s music much loved by her parents.

However, all at school was not so jolly. She had to put up with a lot of racial taunts for a start.

"I was always put down at school," she remembers, "because I am half-Malaysian, half-Scots. I wasn't black and I wasn't white."

Her teachers weren't very nice to her either. At 11 she was, she says, "the teacher's pet" but by 15, it had all gone horribly wrong.

"By the time I was 15 I started going out to nightclubs and missing lessons. I used to be really rude to teachers but I got away with so much."

Alison was also well into dressing up for a lark. She liked the 60s black and white look and recalls "a lot of people said I looked like Natalie Wood (very good-looking actress), so I just started wearing this glamorous look."

Indeed, people were always going on about how she looked like other people, especially the short-skirted, pouting cartoon character from the 30s

called Betty Boop. Alison was quite proud of this one. . .

At 16, she started listening to the super sounds of the underground dance culture, especially rap music. At the same time she'd just started to become big pals with a girl at school called Donna, the only other girl in school who liked hip-hop. At 17 Donna and Alison decided they wanted to start a rap band. They quit their 'A' Level courses, left school, called themselves The She-Rockers and started going to rap concerts instead. They went to see Public Enemy and, after the concert, Alison approached the mean American toughsters in a McDonald's in Shepherd's Bush, and told them they were terrible. Double oh dear. But – hurrah!! – Professor Griff from Public Enemy was impressed enough to ask them all to work together in New York. All was not well however Public Enemy just wanted the girls to do their raps and then leave the

studio. Alison was much miffed. "That really annoyed me," she froths. "It's my music and I must have control over it."

While The She Rockers were living in a house together in New York for a while, the group split up. "I was getting annoyed because people weren't putting the cap on the toothpaste, things like that," she explains. "We just got to dislike each other so much."

Undaunted, Alison returned to London and formed another rap outfit, Hit and Run, but that didn't work out either. She decided to embark on a studio engineering course instead. To this day studio engineers who tell her to "stop touching those knobs!" get a withering glance – quite right too.

Still intent on a rap career Alison approached an independent dance label

called Rhythm King with her super rappings and the label owner was well impressed. He decided she should sing backing vocals on a song called *Hey DJ* by a group called The Beatmasters. It was a massive chart hit, she was signed up by Rhythm King as an artist in her own right, and – bingo!! – the incredibly famed Betty Boo rap star was invented. Then she decided to wear some funny tinfoil clothes. . .

"I'd watch James Bond films and see these sophisticated women. Their style is very simple but it looks powerful and poised. The 60s styles are really

good fun."

But the water-pistol-totin' Betty Boo in the rubber jump-suits is not to be confused with the real Alison Clarkson.

"When I go on stage I'm putting on an act," she clarifies. "It isn't me. I'm quite a withdrawn person most of the time."

Betty Boo's first LP *Boomania* was written in 1990 in six weeks. It was written by Alison completely on her own, in her bedroom in her mum's house, with equipment she bought from the money she made from The Beatmasters record. She is self-taught, self-styled, self-produced and, up until recently, self-managed. "I'm a real bossy boots," she declares. "Bossy Boo, my record company calls me."

Throughout that year she had three massive hit singles from *Boomania*, *Doin' The Do*, *Where Are*

You Baby and *24 Hours*, and became legendary for her videos which featured intergalactic pink polystyrene space craft and the like and disappeared off to America where *Doin' The Do* topped the dance charts in a trice. She soon became an award winner too, winning Best New Act from *Smash Hits* for the whole of 1990. She is now a huge star all over the universe and hardly notices when she's on the front cover of billions of magazines anymore.

She still has big ambitions, too. . . "I'd like to set an example for girls," she says, "and show men that women are capable of producing and writing and

making their own decisions."

She wants to be the new George Michael, too (?).

"He started off as a rapper," she ponders, "he was as young as me when he started. He broke the States, he started his career, he writes his own songs. People say I might turn out like him, I don't know. . ."

BETTY BOO
THE AMAZING FACTS!!

★ She's really scared of lizards!

★ Her boyfriend of a couple of years is called Paul and he's a songwriter: he co-wrote *24 Hours* with Alison.

★ She has quite a lot of brandy to drink whenever she flies because she's so terrified!

★ She was signed up in America by Seymour Stein, the same fellow who signed up Madonna!

★ Her school in Hammersmith was an all-girls school!

★ She recently bought a watch which cost £2,500! Her mum told her off.

★ She has "hundreds of black shoes"!

★ She admits to being quite a jealous person. "I'm possessive about everything," she says, "I get jealous very easily. Or maybe that should be envious, when I'm wishing I could look like someone else. If I didn't have any feelings, I'd be pretty weird."

★ In her spare time she doesn't bother much with clubs and the like, she prefers to stay at home and watch *Coronation Street*!

★ She's quite happy being a sex symbol: "I've always had people telling me I'm attractive, so it doesn't make me feel any different being a pin-up. I look good and there's nothing I can do about that, I was just born that way."

★ She doesn't see herself as perfect, though. "I wish I had a slimmer face," she ponders. "I don't care enough about myself. I've put on weight, but they say when you're 21 all your puppy fat goes and you'll feel a woman." She is now 21!

★ One of her best pals is Lindy Layton from Beats International!

★ She's looking for a place of her own in London.

★ She'd quite like to get married. "When you find the right person the thing to do is marry them and get children. I've found the right person I think. I get all embarrassed talking about it. . ."

★ Her brother is now a DJ!

★ She snores!

★ Sean Connery used to be her granny's milkman before he became famous!

★ She played for an adult netball team when she was 14 and almost took it up as a professional career!

★ She used to play for a five-a-side girls football team!

★ She keeps fit to this day and has the same fitness instructor as Dire Straits, Fleetwood Mac and Boy George!

★ She never does any housework and says when she gets a place of her own she'll get a cleaner in!

★ She has a filofax with all her phone numbers in and her song ideas in scribble form!

★ She uses a cleansing liquid for her face that smells like marzipan!

★ She has a toy puzzle thing called a Bedlam cube.

DJ

SIMON MAYO

"There once was a man called Bono Who didn't like recording in mono He finds he sings best In his pants and his vest With a couple of glasses of Bordeaux."

Full name: Simon "Gazza" Mayo
Date of birth: 29.9.58
Starsign: Libra
Birthplace: Southgate, North London
Height: 6'0"
Weight: 11 stone
Colour of eyes: Blue
Do you have any pets: No.
What qualifications do you have: 7 'O' Levels, 3 'A' Levels, Degree in History and Politics and a bronze fencing medal.
Describe your house: Too small!
What are your parents' jobs: Both retired – my father was a headmaster and my mum a French teacher.
Do you have any brothers and sisters and what are they like: One brother, Jonathon, who's a BBC producer and one sister, Sarah, who's a teacher – they're both lovely people.
Where's your favourite holiday place: Florida.
If you weren't a super DJ, what would you be: A teacher, I suppose, or an inspirational dynamo mid-field player for 'Spurs!
When was the last time you cried and why: When England were knocked out of the World Cup in 1973.
Most embarrassing moment on Top Of The Pops: Introducing the Pet Shop Boys on my very first appearance and not looking at the camera.
Tell us a joke: What does a dyslexic, insomniac, agnostic do? Lies in bed wondering if there is a dog.
Write a poem about your favourite pop star:
There once was a man called Bono
Who didn't like recording in mono
He finds he sings best
In his pants and his vest
With a couple of glasses of Bordeaux.
Do you like yourself: Er. . . not sure about this one!
Do you have a message for the readers: Set your alarm for 6a.m. – and see you at White Hart Lane!

"I never went out with Kylie. . ."

JASON DONOVAN

"On my first day at school I wore a yellow raincoat and hat and I was firing a fake gun. And I was wearing a badge that said 'Jason' on it so all the other kids would know."

"I still run from my house to the gym every day if I can. I don't wear a hat or glasses to disguise myself because I don't want to do that. I've just bought myself a little pushbike actually, so that's how I get around on weekends. I don't really get recognised because I don't think people really expect to see someone like me cycling past."

★

"The people who want to listen to my music will listen to it and if they don't want to, they don't. Nobody's forcing you to listen to this music. Turn the radio off if you don't like it. It's not that painful."

★

"I hate looking at myself in the mirror."

★

"Having a flat in London has made the biggest difference to my life. It sounds quite silly but it's just things like having my own cooking facilities and being able to sit down and watch TV. . ."

"When I look at people's faces when they see me, their faces and their expressions go 'Wow!' and that's fantastic! That's a buzz for me. I've given something to people and made them smile a little bit."

★

"I never went out with Kylie Minogue."

"I probably get along better with females than males."

"I can honestly say I've never felt lonely. Usually the opposite – there are just too many people around."

"In private, I'm probably a little more outrageous than people think I am."

★

"My views are anti-drugs, but it really annoys me when people take such a strong stance against them when alcoholism is a far bigger problem and everyone seems to ignore it."

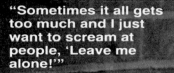

"Sometimes it all gets too much and I just want to scream at people, 'Leave me alone!'"

"I wouldn't say I'm a loner. I'm just a quieter sort of person than most people."

"I've always been known for my white *Hanes* T-shirts and the shirts with the top three buttons undone. I'll wear *Hamnett* pants, but I'll put *Kickers* on and wear white socks over the top of them. Those sort of things are like my own personal stamp."

57

HOW WOULD YOU LIKE TO SPEND A DAY HERE. . . ?

You would, would you? Well, turn the page to find out how. . .

COMPETITION

WIN

A DAY AT TOP OF THE POPS!!!

Yes indeedy! You, your Mum and Dad and a pal of your choosing (i.e. they'd better be nice to you) could be spending an entire day with the Top Of The Pops team! Swirl! into the swankiness that is the new BBC TOTP studio in Elstree, London! Smile sweetly! at the six frantic cameramen as they hurtle about the dance-floor! Shake the very hand! of one of your favourite DJ presenters! Wobble with excitement! at the sight of the chart's hottest stars mouthing the words to their latest hit! Could anything be finer? ("No": A Reader.) And that's not all! because those generous folk at Top Of The Pops have decided to give away piles of groovy stuff — T-shirts, mugs, pens etc etc — to 50 lucky runners-up! Cor! It's a Top Of The Pops Giveaway Jamboree!!!

HOW YOU CAN WIN!!!

It's easy-peasy-lemon-squeezey, people. All you have to do is compose a rap about your favourite pop star, mentioning your favourite pop show (Top Of The Pops of course). It can't be any longer than eight lines, and it must be original. Here's an example for you. . .

Betty Boo is really ace
We all love her smiley face
Her raps are fab, she's just
the tops
Especially on Top Of The
Pops!

Hrrrmmm. Well, you can do a lot better than that, can't you? So why don't you whack down your entry on a postcard and put your full name, age and address on the back and send it to: TOTP Rap Competition, Editorial Department, World International Publishing Ltd., P.O. Box 111, Great Ducie Street, Manchester M60 3BL, to get there no later than 1 February 1992.
There's two age categories: 5 – 10 and 11 – 16, and there'll be one overall winner and 25 runners-up in each age group. Each of the 50 runners-up will receive a fabbo Top Of The Pops T-shirt, a mug, pens and stickers. And the two overall winners will be taking their parents and their pal for a DAY OUT AT TOP OF THE POPS!!

RULES OF ENTRY

1. Entrants must be between the ages of 5 and 16 years old. Entries are limited to one per person.
2. Entries must not exceed eight lines.
3. State your full name, age and address on the back of your entry.
4. All entries will be judged on age and ability. Artistic merit consistent with age of entry will be taken into consideration. The judges' decision is final.
5. The competition is open to residents of the UK only.
6. Employees and their relatives of the BBC, BBC Enterprises, World International Publishing and their respective associated companies are not eligible to enter.
7. No cash alternatives or substitute prizes are available.
8. Winners will be notified by post no later than 1 March 1992. A list of winners' names will be available on request, providing you send a stamped addressed envelope.
9. We regret that no entries can be returned unless accompanied by a stamped addressed envelope.

▲ **Groovy Top Of The Pops Prize Giveaway.**

the end!